MASCOT® BOOKS

Mascot Books
560 Herndon Parkway #120
Herndon, VA 20170
info@mascotbooks.com

PRBVG0715A
ISBN: 978-1-63177-292-4
Library of Congress Control Number: 2015911676

Printed in the United States

www.mascotbooks.com

CHAPTER I

I hardly know where to start with this. I do know this book will not further my status as a writer. I do know it will not fatten my wallet nor be read by those that can. I only hope some of these words find their way to some of these people that want to make a difference. I do know that this is the time something must be done.

The racial uprising in Ferguson, Missouri in 2014 has prompted this. Please excuse the word "uprising", but I can think of no better one. It currently has not been used as it should be. These actions are starting to ricochet across the country and may cause more of the like in other cities.

As in my other writing, there are two sides to every story and this is no different. However, please keep in mind that bigotry is a pathological disorder and not a privilege. It is based in hatred and that, in itself, is a sickness. It is clearly "black versus white," and the huge divide between these two cultures. While it is clearly understood by both sides, it is not clearly understood why. Moreover, during this period of racial unrest, the media continues to address exactly what has happened. To me, they seem to avoid the root cause. This must be addressed and thoroughly discussed.

Fox News Live does a thorough job explaining what should be done. Done to the result with absolutely no concern for the issues as seen by both sides. MSNBC and CNN do a better job, but both adhere closely to the surface of the problem. These major cable news networks do this because "this is where the emotion is." Please remember the Willie Sutton Theory. When asked why he robbed banks, he answered, "Because that is where the money is." This is what sells. This is where the money is, and this is where the ratings are.

That being said, let's try to move on. Studies have proven that cultures are the result of the struggles to exist and to survive in political and societal structures. Our country is the best example because we were put together quickly with every ethnic culture inserted through those east coast funnels. Time and ethnic diversity did not permit long-term cleansing as was found in European cultures.

Of course, near the beginning we brought the slave trade from Africa. Their culture was assembled through a history so completely misunderstood and discarded by the invading white man. We had to remove the Native American to establish a culture so entirely different from the one already cleansed on this continent. The black slave was reduced to a work animal with absolutely no concern for his upbringing and culture. We, the white man, did this with brutal force. We did this because we could. We did this with our culture deeply embedded in our religion and our education. Then we used these two methods to cleanse our misdeeds. This cleansing was done with absolutely no concern or respect for the African or Native American.

I recently read *Bury My Heart At Wounded Knee* by Dee Brown, which contains five hundred pages of the worst atrocities known to man. That is another story that deserves to be told. Dee Brown did an excellent job so let's move on.

This is about black culture as I see it. My wife and I are watching *The Wire*, a five-year series on HBO. Some claim it to be HBO's best. Others see it as the exact opposite, mostly for the reasons mentioned above. My wife and I see it as an excellent portrayal of black culture on the streets of Baltimore. It's not an easy watch, but I highly recommend it for those who wish to improve their understanding of current black culture. To others, this may be a brief synopsis of how we have developed this misunderstanding.

CHAPTER 2

Within a one-month timeframe as the events of Ferguson, on Staten Island we hear of a grand jury doing basically the same thing. The unnecessarily violent restraint of Eric Garner is absolute visual proof supporting the indictment of a white officer causing the death of a black man by illegal force. I tire of constantly writing about the ills of both sides by looking in opposite directions. I write about the so-called "two sides to every story." It is easy to report what is heard and written about this brutality in the media. It is not so easy to delve deeper into areas that may hold some answers.

Let us perceive and set the stage; perhaps search for a cure that may be understood by the ones that can make a difference. It does seem that emotion must be set aside. It also seems that when this is done, a more intellectual approach is necessary; one that doesn't threaten or provoke anger and hate.

Those three words; threaten, anger, and hate, have kept this issue in the forefront of the problem since the first slave arrived on this continent. We, as humans of all colors and creeds, must dig deeper if we are to rise above. We must understand that all people come from different places and have been taught through the circumstances of their roots. As generations pass, these roots become not only stronger, but also more deeply imbedded. As they are imbedded they are taught by elders to be respected. With this they develop meaning and become the standard for living habits. And now a culture is born.

All humans are fundamentally so much alike; we are 99% genetically the same, but we come from different teachings and upbringings. We sift people through these funnels mentioned in the first chapter and superficially believe they are going to think all the same. We set about training them in the ways and means of existing in this country. We do this with laws and acceptable methods as developed by our forefathers. We insist they do things our way. We either forget or do not recognize one very important factor: *our forefathers were white.*

Sure, the black man will become assimilated into this new American culture. Quite frankly, he has done a very good job of this but we, the white man, have not made it easy. As a matter of fact, we have done the opposite. The black man has risen through slavery all the way to the presidency of this country. He has done this in spite of the brutal racial hatred that has been so openly displayed recently in Ferguson and Staten

Island.

We do not call it a black problem when simply it is. It is a problem when the thinking is black *versus* white rather than black *and* white. Personally, I have never liked the words black and white used that way because, in themselves, they are opposites. They too clearly define "them and us." Words; words tell the story. They can either cure this problem, or they can continue to highlight the divisive behavior that causes more white police officers to kill black men.

Oh yes, this will go on. Grand juries will find similar results if words are used as weapons of hate and anger that threaten certain cultures and ways of life founded many years ago out of necessity. This will go on. So will this story as I probe deeper, research my mind or whatever it takes to make steps toward the cure; the cure and not the provocation.

To help set the stage for what is coming, please allow me to express further one of the fears that has provoked this hate and anger; the white man's perceived fear that a black man will rape a white woman, or worse, marry one. This fear has prompted more white atrocities such as lynching than any other. Historically, far more white men have raped black women, and they did it far more openly. But have you ever heard of black men lynching a white man?

CHAPTER 3

In setting this stage, let's take a long look down the black ghettos of today, such as the ones in Baltimore, Philadelphia, D.C., and New York City. The stuff of this day starts here with "corner boys"—young boys who hang out on street corners down deep in the pits of the ghetto. More often than not, these boys come from worn out, dilapidated, and abandoned tenements, much like the places where I was reared. Tenements beyond repair and forgotten about by those politicians that built them.

Corner boys are usually ten to twelve years of age, and some live on the streets if not fortunate enough to live with a parent. This parent, more often than not, is the mother. Fathers move from one woman to the next, as did my father. This is the accepted method of avoiding the responsibility of parenthood. They are there somewhere, but not seen as a parent, nor do they contribute in any way to family.

It is the corner boy's job to hustle business to support himself and perhaps others as well. Today the products of these "businesses" are drugs of varying price and effect, and with an immediate and plentiful market. The corner boys make these profits by spouting off just the way we did with Speakeasies, Tea, Stick, girls, whatever. They are assigned corners by the "Boss Nigga," a term used by local blacks but never safely used by a "whigga"; a whitey. I will steal that license for effect. After all, I am black on the inside, where it counts.

The corner boy is expected to build the trade on his corner and the only way he can do this is with his mouth; using any form of theatrics he can muster to better his income. Should he be lucky enough to be living with his mother, she will encourage his success because this is the only way she can further her income beyond welfare. The most successful corner boys become "runners." When a corner boy makes a sale he calls the runner, who comes in and delivers the product. Then he collects the money after giving the corner boy his "slice." The runner now turns that money over to the Boss Nigga after keeping his "slice." The Boss Nigga has usually aspired through both of the lesser ranks and is favored by the King Pin. The King Pin does not have a title and is seldom seen. He is just like "Hard Head Pete" in my day; heard through others but seldom seen. He rules the hood and his word is law. How is this law practiced? By the Enforcer, or hit man, another player selected for the talent of making people disappear, making them gone. He qualifies for this job by "making his bones" at the order of the King Pin. Not at all different from the methods brought here through Ellis Island so many years ago.

Now back to this so-called "King Pin." He gathers his information from the Boss Nigga when he delivers all of these collections minus his "slice." This person is the ears for what is going on in the streets. The Enforcer is only called in by the King Pin to do his work for one reason; eliminate the snitch. For the sake of this story we can add a couple of bodyguards for this King Pin, usually close relatives. That is the hierarchy. The King Pin accumulates huge piles of cash. He is responsible for keeping the stash houses supplied, and he deals with suppliers outside of the hood. This can be quite hazardous and gives the bodyguards more purpose. It is they who ensure deals for product happen as arranged. Now, what happens to all this cash? Just how much "bling" can you possess? How does it get laundered?

CHAPTER 4

East Side, West Side and all the other sides—these ghettos compete against one another for "supremacy of the perch," as it was called in my day. This competition starts wars; wars cause bodies. Along with the standard, everyday killings, these bodies stack up. They lay about and are cleaned up at the leisure of the system. Should these bodies have some sort of prominence they can be hidden or erased way down in the lowest part of the pit and never seen again. It's the choice of the King Pin, for all these bodies are "on him."

The street cops advise their bosses, who advise the "higher-ups," and then efforts usually wane as politics above determine how this affects the statistics; hereinafter called stats. Stats determine how policing is done in ghettos. Murders and bodies have a big effect on whether police get raises, promotions, or choice duty. If a cop improves the stats by reducing the body count, his boss favors him and then this boss is favored by his boss, all the way to the top. You reduce the body count by just not finding them, even if you do.

Drugs are kept in the forefront of the media by clever conversation with police lieutenants, majors, all the way up to the captain. These officers have risen through the ranks with words; clever words properly and politically used. These words usually paint a better picture by manipulating the stats. This is what the public sees and hears, so far from the actual happening.

Let's now go to street cops with duty in the ghettos. These cops are usually either very dumb and expendable, or very smart and usable; both so necessary for the process. The smart ones and the dumb ones are paid the same, if they are ever paid, because of budget and allocation restraints caused by monetary leakage at the top. Like Willie Sutton, the smart ones know where the money is. They work with and are paid by the Boss Nigga depending on orders and discussion with the King Pin.

If the smart cop does his job well, he is paid extremely well so monies can flow upward through the police system. The dumb ones get a very small slice for cover and subterfuge. They are very expendable. What an opportunity, Mr. Reagan, to advise that money never trickles down. It always trickles up. It always has, and this is nothing more than a fine example. Mario Cuomo advised you in that address he is so remembered for. These are the cities and neighborhoods you choose not to see as you live on that shining mountaintop so far away. Rest in peace, Sir.

Back to the smart street cop. Being that he isn't paid well (or often) by the system, he now has a good income and has created a conduit for huge amounts of money to trickle up through the system. Often he is used to strategically deliver these huge amounts through different forms of launders, and now we have a path beyond the police force. A politician can "push and pull" this money better than anyone because he only operates through (and with) these better-protected connections. He is connected to every method that uses money. Banks, businesses, political contributions and others, all filters for cash to enter the system. This is what happens at the street level.

Let's move on to the King Pin, who may have pallets stacked with cash. For the story's sake and a fine example, let's go to *The Wire*, the HBO series, which is fictional, but only to a certain point. The King Pin, Avon Barksdale, and his sidekick, Stringer Bell, wanted to buy abandoned properties that would soon be sold for development, thus creating huge profits. Stringer dons a business suit, connects himself to a state senator through the police captain, and drops a pallet or two of cash for the purchase of these properties. Now we're doing big business.

Now let's go back to reality. From my youth I saw the value of being connected. It was also known that connections come at a price. What happens when things don't go quite as they were arranged? Arrests are made, because of accidents in the process, for appearances, and sometimes for political punishment. Attorneys need to make a living, too. Where there are attorneys, there are politicians. They are of the same breed. Both carry an abundance of business cards; the standard contract for favors owed. They are passed around to "get out of jail," "dollar amounts owed or due," and as reminders of "what may happen if a promise is broken." The Enforcer is always kept on the ready with a fixed income.

Ah, the power of connections learned at a very young age. Now that we know where the money goes, we also learn how the system protects future earnings and donations; "hush money" better defines it. Should street cops and their immediate bosses appear to be getting strokes of conscience and become less willing to cover the resources, they are readily reassigned to other duties. If that doesn't work, there is plenty of stuff to qualify them for termination. If that still doesn't work, they can switch the allocations of all services from the ghettos to the public schools and walk away slowly until things quiet down. Any or all three usually keeps the corner boys and runners doing what they do best; selling drugs at the retail level.

CHAPTER 5

Now let's bring up schools in the ghettos. Schools with rats running through the corridors, toilets that haven't worked in years. Schools that are usually so under-funded they can hardly exist. Nothing more than a daytime political excuse for the dregs of the teaching profession scared half to death, and themselves possible users of products sold by corner boys.

These kids are parked there by the system until they find a way to escape into the only life they have ever seen; the only world in which they know they can survive. The kids that do go are very young, usually under the corner boy age of ten. Again, usually kids are assigned to these schools by the system and have little to no parenting to qualify them for schooling. Are they dumb? Not at all. They are very smart because they are self-trained by the street to survive. "Smart" in this sense can better be defined as situational awareness.

These young eyes clearly see what is going on around them. They focus on the inevitability of their future. They access their chances and possibilities. They have learned at the hands of other kids to do this because there isn't, nor ever was, a father. More often than not the mother is an addict, a B-Girl hustling at bars, a prostitute, or all three.

Studies have been done by outside sources to develop the levels of intellect for these children, and they are superior, just not in the areas known to white children not raised in ghettos. The parameters are narrow and limited. This parenthesis confines them to a certain way of life. When it comes to a corner craps game, they know how to fade and drag precisely. A white child would not survive in these surroundings nor would they ever qualify to be a corner boy.

If one of these children is born a girl, she is dragged along by the mother into her three trades or perhaps will be lucky enough to be farmed out to relatives a little further up the scale to nowhere. The boys call this "sent to the country," until they develop into material for the three trades. For those who do attend one of these schools in the ghetto, it is here where we begin to see the vast difference in cultures. It is here where black kids live and see what lies ahead. Now, it is also here that white kids, young and old, do not wish to see. They realize the difference is so vast, so undesirable, and so distasteful that they run to the teaching of their parents and teachers in far better neighborhoods. It becomes so apparent, this vast difference in cultures. Should I end this chapter here or should I start the teaching of racial bigotry?

CHAPTER 6

Bigot University, a very easy school to get into, and once you "graduate," it's a flavor that remains at the tip of your tongue and spits out at every opportunity. I never went there but lived around those that did most of my life. I really never even understood why anyone would want to go there, probably because I lived my young years more closely associated with those who were hated; a conglomeration of all skin tones blended into one. If not, it didn't make any difference. We all thought the same way, and our main concern was survival. Survival as a group was easier than surviving alone. I must say here, my thinking hasn't changed much but it has been perfected.

As I have walked and talked through this life, my associations with my fellow man remain the same. There are those that hate, and those that survive, and there is the vast separation between the two. My grandfather taught me this at a very early age. "Get your hand out in friendship first. If the other person does not reach for it, reach for your gun with the other hand and shoot him. He does not want to be your friend and may be reaching for his gun." I believed this to be a humorous lesson rather than a practice, and don't believe my grandfather ever shot anyone. I've been shot at but not hit because of other lessons learned in the streets.

I still practice as written above. I still believe as taught by Martin Luther King, and judge a person by his character and not the color of his skin. It just doesn't make any sense to do otherwise. For me it would be like hating telephone poles, or spoons; how stupid!

That defines my basic thinking. So let's look at other basics. The white man captured, confined, and enslaved the black man. Through the years they have lynched him, burned him out, and fought every measure for him to be treated as an equal. The black man has used every method he could think of to defend himself against this treatment. Then he aspired through every rank to the presidency of this country with little to no help from the white man. Again the basic question, *why should the black man trust the white man*?

The white man continues to use every method possible to keep the black man in a lesser position. The black man continues to better himself against great odds regardless. Why shouldn't the white man be afraid of the black man? The black man has been owned, lynched, shot, beaten, and trod upon by the white man since he has been in this hemisphere. Yet he not only survives, he aspires. He has proven he can do this with intelligence and not violence. Now that is scary, though so very much admired. There we are. The white man is afraid of the black man, mostly for his intelligent methods. The black man doesn't trust the white man. It has taken six chapters to get to these two points; fear and mistrust. What is the cure for these two simple words; words that tend to destroy our country? Words more powerful than bullets.

CHAPTER 7

This chapter is about teaching and understanding clinical bigotry. What, another school? Yeah, here we go with the interesting part. But first let's take a look at what rests in between the two words fear and trust. This is truly my observation. Yes, another two words; hatred and anger. Yes, the white man is mad. This has been my experience for as long as I can remember.

Of course, as a result of this book I studied further because racism is an indispensable part of capitalism. It has always been one of the most important ways of keeping lesser classes down and in their place, powerless in a capitalistic state. Are racism and bigotry illegal? Of course they are, and laws have been in place going back to the days of Lincoln. We twist or ignore them in a time of greedy need. This is not done in other countries.

So let's move on to the clinical diagnosis. This is not just a current study by me. This is history and so much is written and practiced in the mental health community. Yes, it is a delusional disorder; a major psychiatric illness of a negative and pejorative nature that can lead to extreme murderous behavior. That should be enough to handle Ferguson and Staten Island.

Okay, I've calmed down so let's move on. I'm not a psychiatrist or a professional of any sort. I have studied clinical drug and alcohol rehabilitation and what happens in extreme cases. It's not a pretty picture, but similarity rears its ugly head with the terms of schizophrenia, bipolar, and other very serious mental disorders. I can link them, the medical profession can link them, and the psychiatric profession can link them. *Why can't the legal profession link them*?

In my opinion, the answer must lie in our greedy capitalistic political structure. My personal belief is that the "ugly head" rests here. "We've got to keep certain people in their place so money can trickle up." This is not an actual quote, but something that is so accurately displayed within the drug culture.

Now we will go back to Willie Sutton's declaration of, "That's where the money is." The money is at the top and they're going to keep it flowing. Once the money flows to the top it can easily be invested and protected by the "laws" of the white man. This, too, has been going on for as long as I can remember. A good example of this is our stock market. How does the public deal with it? How does the public exist within this structure? How do we live with this fear and hatred? The ways and means are hidden within the reason for this book; BIGOTRY.

CHAPTER 8

Another not-so-pretty picture will be painted here. We have killed off thousands of Native Americans, stolen their land and confined them to reservations, most of which are not unlike ghettos. Black ghettos have been built on the depravity of racism and bigotry. Then we find a way to profit off of them with the drug culture. Then we twist our laws with political capitalism to keep the money flowing to the top. We do this with symbolic gestures that resemble efforts that will lead to a prosperous result, but these often fail hopelessly when the politician leaves the podium.

Yes, we're good at this kind of stuff as we criticize other countries for their political structure. It's not that I necessarily agree with other methods. It's that I think we should concentrate on our own. We simply forget that we stand on the shoulders on our ancestors: Europeans, slaves, and Native Americans, without whom we would not even exist. What did exist was the need for one another. The need to share our lives and build on the result: democracy—a form of freedom that provides for all.

When did greed take this over? Yes, I think I know; the likes of the DuPonts, Vanderbilts, Carnegies, and Rockefellers are responsible. This is not to say that these were necessarily bad people. These wealthy families introduced the "more is better" thinking, and then they took it to the extreme. They took capitalism to the extreme. As they did this, others found ways to emulate this kind of life. Then more ways were found to accumulate huge wealth. Then the big bust came and people jumped out of windows because they couldn't perceive any other way of life. Then the drug of my choice, booze, was outlawed with the Volstead Act.

Yes, outlawed things bring "outlaws," and what a school this was; not too different from the drugs of today. If you have the guts to do it, even the lowest dregs of life can make money. As they make this money, the loot becomes visible to the chain upward. Then the fun and games start just as they did throughout my childhood. The product of today is not liquid and that is about the only difference.

The huge illegal profits create greed. To experience this greed, it is necessary to make these huge profits appear legal. The masters of this, the politicians, control the system. As a result, the loot trickles upward. It's simple, really—just ask Joe Kennedy and the like. You cannot keep a politician's fingers out of this money. It is the lifeblood of their existence. Without it, they would be honest men. Honest men are not politicians.

A few honest men may hold public office and may even aspire to the top, but they are not liked, and every effort will be made to destroy them by politicians. Just ask Barack Obama; that's another story.

Let's get back to the huge amounts of illegal money finding its way upward as they spout about the theory of their hero, Ronald Reagan. Reagan wanted to take care of the poor working class with his trickle down chatter. Please allow me to borrow part of a quote from Thomas Carlyle. Please allow me to politicize it so he would be ashamed of it: "He who has health has hope. He who has hope has everything." Now let me add, "He who has wealth does not need hope. He can buy what is needed: a politician."

I will end this chapter, as it might appear I'm stretching close to the top, or maybe a bit over the top. I chose to do this to brighten this portrait so I may keep you interested in a topic that may be avoided by those who may otherwise do so.

CHAPTER 9

The more I read and research about racial hatred, the more it seems it leads to pathological bigotry. While it is true that hatred is suffered by most, the argument remains; when does it become irrational? To me, this is when the one that hates justifies his or her hatred with an action. A physical action is self-explanatory and clarifies the diagnosis of a mental disorder. An action may only be in words.

While words can be very damaging, they create more words that try to justify the action. Now we have an argument that, in itself, leads to an action. And here we are with pathological bigotry. Should these words include "danger to self or others" in any manner, we are well into what may require treatment.

Ignorance can be used to defend this disorder. "This is the way I was brought up," or "this is the way it is," are some examples of ignorance. Quotes like these can go on and on, and they are usually thought of by the academic and intellectual communities as human stupidity. Human stupidity cannot be treated as a mental disorder by law, or so I'm told. In one of my books I quoted the comedian Ron White, with one of his best: "you can't fix stupid."

Wouldn't it be nice if we could end this conversation there? Sadly though, we cannot end it there. Fear of bigotry being used by the legal system deters political action to make changes. If you listen to what I do—in the media—racial hatred, bigotry and prejudice, coded or not, create huge political contributions and donations. This type of conversation is so cleverly laced into political direction that it has divided our country to the point of being dangerous. Ferguson and Staten Island incidences certainly qualify this. Yet, we go into lengthy grand jury decisions that have only further divided our country.

Trayvon Martin, the young, unarmed black man shot by a white man, and others are brought back into the conversation to further this unrest. What has been written in this chapter has been done for one reason. Please remember what was written in chapter 7. We could be well on the way to the cure if it wasn't for the law, the legal profession, and politicians. Research clearly supports that the solution lies within the confines of the psychiatric and medical professions.

Studies go on and on by the most academic intellectuals, yet the law favors and protects the ignorance of pathological bigotry. If our country was founded on laws, and should all people be treated equally under the law, we are surely headed in the wrong direction. What will it take to change this direction?

CHAPTER 10

I just finished listening to commentary on the laws of grand juries. Of course, this relates to the current two laws made as a result of Ferguson and Staten Island. The varying derivatives of these legal practices left me in a complete state of confusion. I'm not a lawyer, but I have been involved in many legal processes. It is ridiculous to think a layperson at one of these juries could understand or even come to a conclusive thought in order to arrive at a decision. Moreover, a clever legal presenter could easily reverse the decision of a witness should things not be going in the predefined direction.

This is just one instance of what has happened to the manipulation of our legal system. Remember the famous saying from the O.J. Simpson trial, "if the glove doesn't fit, you must acquit." Just who do we think committed those murders? Sure, our country was founded on laws, and we all should practice within certain guidelines so everyone will be treated fairly and justly.

President Obama, who has the highest honors at Harvard for Constitutional Law, said in a recent speech: "all should be treated equal under the law." It is felt that he truly believes this, but "should" is a funny word, and he truly believes that also. His words have been twisted, disrespected, and slandered since he has been president. The best of thinkers conclude the underlying reason is because he is black.

Here we are, on the merry-go-round of law. Over the years I have studied tax laws, mostly for the same reason as those that manipulate the laws in order to pay less. It is so often said, the smarter the tax lawyer, the less your taxes will be. This is why half of our monetary capital is held in tax havens. *How else*?

Please allow me to wander off in the reasoning of this. This earth was designed to be self-perpetuating and God probably did this. He put all the living creatures on this earth to assist in this perpetuation. One of these creatures was man, and this man seemed to be a better thinker than the other animals. Man assumed he had a better relationship with God and started writing about it. In his interpretation he designed for himself a superior authority over all other creatures. And life went on.

All the animals, birds, and fish alike saw that the forests, lakes, rivers, and oceans were kept clean and able so they would continue sustaining nature. Man saw differently and started inventing better ways for him to aspire. This aspiration led to competition, and man started inventing ways in which he could live better than other men; a competition that led to greed.

Greed caused wars and other forms of destruction causing our forests, lakes, rivers, and oceans to become dirty and unable to sustain themselves. This has caused certain animals, birds and fish to die off and become extinct. Man not only continues to perpetuate—he manipulates the system to create more men than we have room for. He does this mostly with words, and these words lead to methods, and some of these methods become law. Do you like apples? How do you like those apples? A quote from *Good Will Hunting*.

CHAPTER II

As I have written before, this country has slowly turned itself into an oligarchy. As you would imagine, I would study further. As you might have guessed, we are one. These studies by universities and political scientists now conclude that our system of government is best defined as an oligarchy. It's all over the Internet and you can gather information that leads to a pyramid of the elite few that control our so-called democracy. This was clearly defined by the last mid-term election.

The controlling political system serves the elite special interests and not the people. Our government does not represent the majority of the citizens of this country; rather, it represents the elite few. This is not me telling you this time. It is universities such as Princeton and Northwestern. The Supreme Court has decided that wealthy donors can contribute as much as they want to political campaigns. It is here and only here where elections are controlled, or should I say, bought.

Again, just ask Willie Sutton. This is where the money is and all a greedy politician must do is ask for it. Willie broke the law; the politician makes the law. Of course, his soul has been purchased along with his mouth. The artful twisting of words is arranged for them by the best of writers. I am a piker by comparison. I read, listen, and gather my thoughts, and get no contributions. I do this so all may reflect on the situation of our country drifting toward the destruction caused by the greed of a few.

This disease is now becoming clearer. A cure cannot be researched until you isolate the cause. Are you as surprised as I am to realize that by isolating those at the top, those not so many elite few, a cure can be started? Again, allow me to wander off in this direction. We gather up all these diseased people and take them to an island colony. They may bring all of what caused this disease with them. In order for them to start on the road to recovery they allow us, by law, to bundle it all up in one big mass of money and pay off our national debt. You say we have a whole lot left over? We build new roads and bridges, clean up our water supply, and reforest. Still some more left over? Let's give the young student a break and pay off educational debt.

We're getting close now. We build a mental hospital on this island and every time we see a politician reach for political campaign funds we send him in this direction. We send for the helicopter ambulance and send him directly to this island to be cured.

As mentioned above, this disease must have continuing research contributions to further the study of the cure for greed. Finding these funds will not be difficult now because we all know how it originates. And yes, over time this mental hospital will become more self-sustaining as word will get out through our media. They will be anxious to advise how nice life is when all have enough to live peacefully with not too much, just enough to know the importance of not being greedy. Life will be great on this earth-all but on this island; this mental hospital for the elite greedy few. Funny thing about all this; a guy named Jesus had the cure a couple of thousand years ago. He didn't need islands or mental hospitals. He did it just with words.

CHAPTER 12

Let's discuss two facets of our system—Democrats and Republicans. One so big it gets lost in the humanistic state of greed. One so small it can sell its humanistic state of greed to the elite few. This is a pessimistic view seen by too many of the voting public. And there it is again, a part of the cure. Realistically the voting public has control of a big part of the problem. Now we get lost in trying to cure them, or better stated would be to educate them. Education would sure make a big dent in the cure. Idealistically, government shouldn't be too big or too small. Greed can cause either. Take greed out of the picture and the illness of size cures itself. To perpetuate greed you must encompass most of the bad side of being human. Fancier words could be used here, but putting lipstick on a pig still leaves you with a pig.

Greed is like a product being sold to and consumed by the buyer; don't buy it, and you don't have it. Like any other drug, the more of it you buy and use, the more you want to buy and use. You were not born with it. It is something you bought into along the way.

What is greed? Mostly it is about wanting more than my share and not caring how I get it. Like drugs, greed is sold by convincing someone you can make them feel better for a price. What you don't tell them is feeling better only lasts for a very short period. Put simply, if you can be emotionally manipulated, mentally, physically, or psychologically you are buying into a product that will eventually make the seller more than you are getting.

If you need to put someone down to elevate how you feel about yourself, the feeling will have a short lifespan. If you want to feel good about yourself you must earn it. You cannot buy it.

And now we will cover bigotry, prejudice, and racism. It is something you bought along the way. It is something you need to buy in to as you grow. It is something sold to you so you can think you are better than someone else. In order for you to beat the drum of this disorder, you must belong to a select group. Those that sell it to you collect the price of belonging to this group. In some way or another they collect because racism is a part of greed and greed is a huge part of elitism.

Now we have the chain upward to that select group. The problem is, you cannot be an elite if they have all your money. This is where we separate the ignorant racist from the smart racist. The smart racist has used you to attain his elite status and he will continue doing this by selling you more of what you think will get you there. In fact, it only keeps you exactly where he wants you; paying so you can continue feeling better than someone you probably have never met. When you play his game, you have just bought in to the hate game. How do you feel now?

CHAPTER 13

Have you noticed how often greed appears in this book? It is not a pretty word and it is danced around by the media but seldom used. If we are to step up and face the current living situation in this country, however, it must be used. Now that some of the greatest thinkers have analyzed the direction of our economy it must be shouted from every rooftop. You cannot call us an oligarchy without saying it was caused by greed. So let's move on to what is happening.

Now that these monstrously huge multinational corporations tell our government leaders how to run this country, we must define what to call the people that use their products. Yes, all the while we thought we were participants of this great democracy when we actually were nothing more than consumers. We have over-populated our country because we weren't smart like the Chinese, who formed a "nookie police."

As a result, our leader corporations are burdened with only producing trash products that can be afforded, which are hawked by another leader corporation called the media. We purchase these junk products and our living standards decrease, and ghettos and crumbling neighborhoods spawn. Minimum wage jobs are the only ones available because the consumer is without any power to make the necessary changes. When this happens, the smarter residents find ways to profit within these neighborhoods. Now we have a whole new method of climbing the socio-economic ladder.

Drugs originated in this underground step upward, as did booze in the Roaring Twenties. And what an "infant and emerging economy" this is. Huge profits that have absolutely nothing to do with improving living conditions are being made in these slums. As a matter of fact, they deter it. Being that our governing officials have surrendered power to the monster corporations, they identify with these huge profits in the drug trade. Through the already mentioned mastery of twisted law talk, the "trickle upward" of these illegal profits find their way into the pockets of politicians. Now the monster corporations see profits fall toward a recessionary economy.

Being that they are the ones with the real power, they can easily convince politicians through more of this twisted law talk to subsidize their waning profits. After all, they are too big to fail. So the politician zaps the tax bucket to keep them happily subsidized. When this happens, taxes must be raised on the ones that pay them. Can this be done to the monster corporations? Hell no! The corporations took care of that years ago with loopholes and tax havens. And there you are, just look around. Close your eyes—see it? Now open them and look at our roads, bridges and schools. Look at the countryside. Our rivers and oceans are littered with tons of discarded plastics and other trash. *How did this happen to us in this great country*?

CHAPTER 14

Let's go back to the Clinton days, when Greenspan was re-reading the ways of Ayn Rand. Going back to the days of NAFTA, we thought this global economy was the way to go. This would open markets never tapped before. We could unload our excesses "over there," and a huge amount of profit would flow into the US. The expansion of free marketing would have a better chance of proving itself.

George H.W. Bush was so pleased when Bill Clinton signed his bill into law that it went in to effect on January 1, 1994. President Clinton was truly convinced that if he signed this thing without protecting the

American worker, it would create jobs. Now we have twenty years of listening to the "giant sucking sound"; the battle cry of Ross Perot. Bill Clinton was absolutely right about this.

First, it created these jobs in Canada and Mexico with auto manufacturing and fruit and vegetable production in Mexico. Then these two adjoining countries taught China and India the many advantages of this merging industrialization. And there we go making Mr. Perot so right that he will never be forgotten for those three words.

And here we are with these huge corporations trying to find ways to increase profits, first by the exportation of products, and second by forming subsidiary arms in these countries to manufacture them. Did NAFTA work? Absolutely. We saw huge profits and many jobs created—just not for our working middle class. As we hobble along, we continue to listen to President Obama with these brilliant plans of hope and change. Yes, he thought this may be possible and yes, he thought the people would support these ideas. Again, he was right to think so.

Where he was wrong was failing to realize that the people no longer have the power of the vote. The corporations own this too. This was so proven with the last mid-term elections. It is my understanding, and studies have concluded, that our governmental policies rarely align with the majority of the people. They align with the elite few at the top. The ones who live in mansions, have doctors on call for healthcare, and get about in private jets. This can only be defined as an oligarchy.

Oligarchies are nice for the very few at the top but they do not last. Just ask President Putin, who is approaching the personal net worth of Bill Gates. I just hope not too much is tied up in the Russian Ruble. Have you been watching the current money market? It's not a pretty picture for

Vladimir. Shirtless swagger doesn't count here, even though it is much admired by Rudy Giuliani and few other conservatives.

It is hard to believe Russia exceeds Saudi Arabia in oil production. It does, but the balance sheets are not the same. Saudi Arabia can afford to watch oil by the barrel drop in price. Putin can't, and he had better watch his neighbors. Part of the euro is based on the ruble. Not only that, he has borrowed deeply into the pockets of these neighbors. You can take your stack and hide behind the well-guarded gates of your compound, but no one will see you riding your horse without a shirt on—not even Rudy Giuliani.

CHAPTER 15

Where are we going with all this? What has all this got to do with finding a cure for bigotry? Please allow me the license to paint a picture of how all of this negativism contributes to the direction of the average American citizen. This person takes his hard-earned minimum wage to Wal-Mart and deals with its employees who are making the same minimum wage hawking products made in every country but ours.

Look at the people at the top; good old (but dead) Sam Walton's relatives, who average about $30 million per year. Thirty million, and they do absolutely nothing to earn it. Alice Walton buys fancy sport cars, drives them carelessly while drinking heavily, and smashes them hopelessly, with one count of vehicular homicide to her credit. I'm told the Walton family is the richest family in this country. I'm also told they are the greediest, giving just 0.04% of their earnings to charity with a total net worth of over $140 billion.

I had the opportunity to wander through the hills of Bentonville, Arkansas and gaze at the Crystal Bridges museum from afar with little desire to see what is inside. I understand Alice has had quite a bit of fun collecting American art as she sees it. That's life as Alice sees it. Do you think her vision is one that contributes to the betterment of the thousands of Wal-Mart employees? These full-time employees must get food stamps and other assistance just to survive. Do you think this vision contributes to *anything* other than Alice?

Sure, all this money is hers, as it is with the rest of the Walton family, but my questions are simple: wasn't all this money made in this country? Didn't our free-market legal system make this possible? Didn't all those employees from top to bottom contribute to making this fortune? Isn't this greed? Warren Buffet and Bill Gates have given a third of their wealth to charity or to assist those in need. These are very rich people who made this wealth themselves. See the difference? Feel the difference?

Maybe a free market system would work if we could eliminate greed. Just how would you go about that without some form of regulation? Sounds impossible doesn't it? Please be advised that it isn't, and we have been almost there in the past. Regulation and taxation is clearly defined at the top, before the money is made. It is only the twisting of tax laws by legislation that has changed them to favor the elite. Should these huge profits be used for charity or the betterment of employees, they become tax deductible. Simple, isn't it?

What is the purpose of government? It is to protect and regulate. To govern; to preside over the people they were elected to protect and regulate. Regulation is the law that protects people from economic manipulation by those with more power. Markets can be free, with free defined as freedom for all people treated equally under the law. Can't you picture lawyers getting a hold of those last few sentences and twisting them into a stack of paper ten inches thick?

CHAPTER 16

Somewhere in the twelfth century an Englishman came up with the Magna Carta. This came into being so the King would have to treat the commoner fairly. The commoner would have his chance in court to be treated this way. About 400 years later, someone came up with Habeas Corpus which, as I understand it, has about the same meaning and effect as the Magna Carta. Habeas corpus is nothing but a legal procedure stating that a prisoner has the right to be treated justly in court.

Not that I have much interest in those historic writings, but they do reflect on the freedom of the lower classes, like the workers, the peons, the ones that actually do something. Those workers kept the feudal lords and royalties from taking all the fruits of the land. Then, during the next five or six centuries, a baseline was formed to determine the meaning of freedom. The hierarchy owned the land and felt they should be compensated for its use. Everyone else had no place to live other than on this land. Do you see what's coming? A need for someone to arbitrate this without sword in hand? And now we're blessed with laws, which you can't have without... lawyers.

So certain people were selected and they became great barristers and the game was on. What a wonderful position this was because they could tell kings, lords, and such how things "should be." Of course they told the rest what "would be." After deciding how the lawyers should be paid and who could afford to pay them, the necessity of taxations and rents were established. Do you think it necessary to go into whom these discussions were with? Didn't think so. The aforementioned "would be" now becomes law. And there you are; that is how the need for these lawyers arose.

Yes, we have great barristers and lawyers. We also have the sort such as Saul from *Breaking Bad*. What a great profession this has become over all these years. Huge law schools pump them out in huge quantities because they are the ones that get to tell all the rest of us how it "should be" or would be." Ain't that nice!

Well it was, until lawyers starting telling other lawyers how it should or would be. It was another huge battle that resulted in the formation of politicians. Politicians are what lawyers used to be. And here we are again at this great arbitration deciding who has the most power to determine what should be or would be.

CHAPTER 17

Let's step forward from that last historical synopsis sketching briefly my opinion of our legal system. Going back all those years, we did learn the necessity of taxation. We mammals have learned that as alpha types, we will always have leaders of the pack.

Somebody is always going to rule the roost, so we're quite fortunate to do this by election. Please don't ask my opinion of our system at this time—just be grateful we still can vote. These leaders must tax the pack for this governing protection. That being established, we will step forward.

Ronald Reagan spouted that deficits are not important. Dick

Cheney continued this chant all the way up through the Bush years. George H.W. Bush continued with these thoughts just like Ronnie did. Clinton heard, but not enough. It only became a bad thing when it was passed on to President Obama.

Republican Speaker Boehner makes such noise about how this president is casting our country to the wolves with all this debt. The monstrously huge corporations, you know those job creators will be expected to pay higher taxes. This will ruin the entire free market system. Higher tax for the rich is the damnation of the Grand Old Party. It is preached every night on Fox News Live. Forbes prints a magazine that is biblical to the rich and famous.

These riches for the huge corporations are stored in offshore tax havens. Please allow me to call them taxes, for that is what they were or should be. They are now called profits arranged by clever tax lawyers with magical loopholes to sell. If this money were employed in this country to rebuild our crumbling roads, bridges, and schools, we would not have to look at crumbling roads, bridges, and schools.

It is my understanding that this amount equals the entire economy of the country. Half of our work force works for minimum wage and cannot sustain a livelihood without food stamps, etc. We have one of the worst healthcare systems in the world. A night out for a family of four means a trip to Hardee's for a fried bologna and Velveeta biscuit. As we watch our country fall apart for just about everyone except the very few rich, we ponder how other countries deal with this.

Let's look at Denmark, this nice little Scandinavian country that seldom gets talked about on the evening news or magazines. There, no one complains about taxes, no one complains about the government, and no one works more than 40 hours per week. They get a month of vacation every year, and excellent healthcare is free for life. For this, they pay about thirty percent of their income in taxes and love every minute of it. They have no trouble buying a home, a car or two, and a decent, happy family life is a reality for anyone that chooses it. Whites and blacks live at the same standard and gays have been able to marry since 1978.

When is the last time you heard of a Dane asking for asylum in this country? You might also ask a Swede, a Finn, a Norwegian, or anyone else living in that neck of the woods if taxes are a bad thing. Taxes actually enable them to be very happy and well cared for, with the lowest illiteracy rate in the world. Of course, they all recognize that capital is the human structure of their country and not necessarily wealth. Therefore, money is poured into educating the young and is considered the best possible investment for a prosperous and content country.

CHAPTER 18

Somewhere along this road the wheels fell off our wagon and we went over a huge cliff into a new world of thinking. My grandfather, Earnest John Kohler, who was brought up an orphan in Germany taught me the following: "Our good God and family said, 'we are all brothers and therefore we are our brother's keeper.'" I'm now eighty-four, and for the life of me, this still rings true and I want to live my life that way. Others say, "good God and country said to them, 'others are not my brothers and they should look after themselves'"—as they did.

From this, they gather that if you can afford slaves, you should buy them. If you can afford an easier and better life for yourself, you should buy it. If anything is left over at the end of life, give it to your lazy, undereducated adult kid to do with as he wishes, just like Alice Walton is doing. And from that we find our country in its present state. Little to no concern is given that others are the lawful prey of anyone having more power, financial or otherwise.

Now go back to Alice Walton and compare her to Warren Buffet and Bill Gates. Somewhere in that thinking is this huge cliff that we, the American people, have fallen over. Warren Buffet and Bill Gates started this race through life so far back from Alice Walton that she has no idea of where she started.

This country's system is based solely on capitalism; materialistic capitalism. Our leaders tell us freedom is based on capitalism. We are free to make as much as we want, and we can spend it any way we choose. What we are witnessing now is the result. We have the wealth; we have the power. We had the resources as we watched our country crumble. Why is it so hard to see why this is happening? Can't we see that we are wasting our most precious resource; young people waiting to be educated on how to better our country? The people who recognize this are the resource; the leaders aren't. Our leaders are just gathering wealth and power. The more wealth and power a person has, the easier it is to gather more. *That* is capitalism in America. Money makes money; people don't.

CHAPTER 19

It is such a shame that we do not see this. If we ever come to our senses and realize that people are far more important than money, we may still have a chance to survive. My wife Marilyn says that it must be generational ignorance. I agree, and add that it must be generational ignorance gone mad because we are self-destructing. We have been doing this for so many years that our governing system cannot see the accelerating pace. I think this is because of greed. This is best exemplified by the lifestyles and incomes they have arranged for themselves.

All these natural resources we have are available, just in the wrong place. If only we could see what would happen if we place more importance on people than we do money, we just may be able to change direction toward self-perpetuation. If we don't, the acceleration is only a generation or two from nipping at our heels.

During the last presidential campaign, it was shouted from every GOP rooftop that we needed Donald Trump or Mitt Romney to win because they understood business. What terrible thinking. These monstrously huge companies were founded on this thinking and now they want that to expand. This is not brilliance. This is not even smart. Both of the aforementioned people started with such a huge inheritance that they kept betting on sure things that their fathers created. You could almost say our present political thinking insured these winnings. Again, money makes money; people don't.

Like Alice Walton, Trump and Romney are two more names added to the list of what can happen when this money is spent on mansions and not reinvested in the real capital of this country; our people. People must make money by producing products and methods that will advance the education of all people.

Believe it or not, this can be done within a free market society. We must be smart enough to understand the meaning of those two words. They do not mean "grab as much as you can for yourself and screw the rest." Free market means that you must work hard to keep it free and self-perpetuating. This means the market must be kept free of greed, free of corruption, free of manipulating the profits for self-need. Can this be done? Sure it can be done, just remove those three words from our political structure; greed, corruption, and manipulation.

How do you do this? Of course, one way is to never do these things in the first place, like the Scandinavian countries. But, I'm afraid that ship has sailed. We are rapidly going in the wrong direction. We did not listen to President Obama. We fought tooth and nail against his philosophy of change. The GOP continues with every thread of its being to destroy this kind of thinking. They are just not smart enough to see that when money makes money, you eventually end up with a big stack of money, *but with no people.*

CHAPTER 20

Now that we have built this "house of cards" and all this monetary wealth has been passed on to the few at the top, our political leaders still find ways to manipulate enough votes to continue. Our last mid-term election confirmed this. Being that the GOP Congress has found ways to keep their voters ignorant (dumbed down) and the opposing voters from the poles by manipulating them along with the registration rules, the worth of our country dwindles. They continue to find twisted methods of keeping the money flowing to the top. Doesn't this have a certain "smell"? If nothing else, it should have an odor of tainted politics, even to Republicans.

President Reagan, you should roll over in your grave and take a look now. Just take a look at what trickle down started. Thank you, Ronnie. I am speaking to voters now. Is this okay with you? Is this the way you want your leaders to run things? Is it simply about putting up with anything to discredit and disrespect our black president? Do you hate him that much? Recently, in Mountain Home, Arkansas, the windows of a Unitarian church were shot out and these words were prominently left to explain: "to Mr. Billy Bob, from your neighbors. You filthy white trash scum Billy. Why don't you move to Ferguson, MO or Chi-Congo, IL since you like niggers and queers so well. And as you idolize the nigger commie, muslin, scholiast, destroying the USA. He is the worst garbage to ever occupy the White House bar none. See how long your white trash ass would last among them, you brain dead bastard. Just remember, we true southerners know where you live, asshole!"

That is a direct quote from a picture taken at this church. I have a copy with incorrect spelling and all. If this doesn't paint the exact picture of this hatred-laced ignorance, nothing will. Has this been reported to the police and other authorities? Yes. What has been done? Nothing. Why? Please read the above and do not stop until you get to the end of this book. It appears we, as a country, find this to be acceptable behavior. Personally, I am sickened by it, and I think it clearly defines what is wrong. It clearly defines our attitude toward it. We have allowed this sickness to be firmly imbedded in our culture. That one letter is so explosive with racial and bigoted hatred it is impossible to see a safe return to sanity for those responsible. Yet, we have done nothing about it as a country.

As a matter of fact, Speaker of the House Boehner, the Republican-controlled Congress, Rush Limbaugh, and the gang at Fox News Live spout covert and direct messages daily that encourage this thinking and these actions. These people are educating their constituents to think this way. Are they not the teachers of this behavior? Are they not responsible?

Now remember what was said at the beginning of this book? Remember the one word that was missed along the way? The word is *cure*. Feel it coming?

CHAPTER 21

I just read the book *Threshold* by Thom Hartmann, a brilliant and eloquent author. This book is about a progressive plan to pull America back from the brink of failure. Early in the book he uses Maslow's Hierarchy of Needs to explain what happens as the assets of a country trickle up.

Imagine a triangle with three equal sides. Now imagine a horizontal line about halfway up. We'll call this line the threshold. See the volume in both portions? As this line, which we now call the wealth threshold, moves upward, the top volume becomes lesser. The volume at the bottom represents all of us working, producing, and creating profits.

As the wealthy gain more of these profits by paying us less and keeping these profits for themselves, we grow more in numbers but with less in our pockets. Get the picture? Was this painted well? At this juncture, right here in our country, can you picture where this threshold line now is?

Now consider the acceleration of this line moving upward and allow me to thank Mr. Hartmann for this plagiarism. Allow me also to plagiarize another great thinker, Bernie Madoff. Somewhere along the way as he twisted the system and hid away the secrets of stashing all this wealth he had to know there would be an end. He also had to know that the more he did it, the quicker it would happen. He is now serving 150 years in prison for this thinking. Here we paint a picture of two great thinkers about wealth; one is for the people, the other is for himself. One is free to continue, the other isn't.

While this is an interesting little synopsis, it is only meant to indicate the acceleration of the trickling up of the assets of our country. This usually implies that there will be an end, as it was for Ponzi and Madoff. Oh yeah, I'm getting closer to the cure. I don't really mean to be teasing you, but in order to complete a painting of all the details, some unattractive colors must be included. In order to solve a mystery all the characters, good and bad, must be profiled. How the "way to go" differs from the way we are going becomes more explicit.

CHAPTER 22

As the few at the top drain away the assets of this country and stash them elsewhere for future use, someone may figure how to get this money back into play right here in our country. It is my understanding that Warren Buffet and Bill Gates had quite a talk with President Obama. They are suggesting that other multi-billionaires assign the future use of their wealth to some form of charity.

Everybody wins when this is done. First, they receive huge tax deductions. Next, they can continue investing this money and enjoy the profits. Then, the assignees can borrow against these funds for present needs. Great idea except we, as a country, can't accept charity as such. We, at least, have the "as such" to work on, and believe me; it's got me thinking. All that dormant tax haven money could come into play here. It's not being used or taxed. It's not being borrowed and all we need is cooperative wealthy people and companies. Now, that's the hard part.

My personal thinking is let us borrow the money and not pay interest. Every dollar borrowed is now tax-free. As we invest this money in our people to build roads, bridges, schools, etc., and improve the industrial thinking of this country, someday down the road, we will repay the rich lender with tax-free dollars.

We can memorialize this borrowing with bonds, treasury notes, whatever. The rich can stay rich; people will be back to work making a decent wage and up to half of this country's monetary system is back in play. Not possible, you say? Why not? All it would take is Americans becoming American again. Re-create the thinking that we are all in this thing together. The assets, people, and wealth are here. Those two things are in good shape. It's our thinking that is screwed up. Let me rephrase that; it is the thinking of our governing thinkers that is screwed up.

Before we can re-educate the people, we must re-educate government. How do you go about that? I am getting closer! Remember a quote by Whoopee Goldberg? "Let me hold the light while you find a better way." I'm willing to do that. The people are willing to do that, and the rich people could go to the country club and boast about all of these bonds and notes they have in hand while they rebuild America.

Sure, we're creating the likes of the Vanderbilts, Astors, DuPonts, and the like. That's okay with me. They have their mansions and the income to presently support them. We're just using what they're not using.

Now, when they die off and their kids aren't smart enough to see what we have done, they can donate these mansions to the government for museums. Everybody wins. Dream on, Edward. It is from dreams that great happenings are seeded.

CHAPTER 23

Let's get on with this insidious, tyrannical behavior. Let's delve into the connection between bigotry and greed. To me they are closely entwined. Both are used to elevate the self above others through some form of leverage so that the self can feel better than others. It is a narcissistic personality disorder to control others by placing them in a lesser status. In those words I am finding it hard to find the patriotic American, yet every greedy bigot claims to be one. This is being used to define what certain politicians are saying in certain churches. What went on in Mountain Home, Arkansas is a good example. Yet, these people can easily get all tangled up in the reasons for capitalism and a free market system.

Now we are off and running toward the purpose of this book. As we look back over our history we can see so many incidences for and against this behavior. In a capitalistic state we inspire people to study more, work hard, and get ahead.

In a free market system this is possible because you make a product, provide a service, and charge a price for whatever the market will bear. You are free to do this. You are free to work hard. You are free to study. Whoops! The first bumps in this theory occur.

Why are some people free to study in better schools, with better teachers, and with the best accoutrements? Why do some who have been to these schools work less, get paid more, and continue to get better accouterments? And there you are. Some start the race through life way out in front of others. Seldom in my life have I met many that started way out there in front that didn't think they were better than others. The hard part to swallow is that they probably are. They probably are better because of the better schools, better teachers, and better accouterments.

In this country the law says we are all to be treated equally. This is not a precise example that I have written here, it is just one that indicates that laws must continually be governed and regulated. This is exactly what the GOP continually argues against. They insist on smaller government and less regulation. As did Gordon Gekko of Wall Street fame when he said, "greed is good." Of course, he was a fictional character.

Ivan Boesky and Michael Milken were both the real thing and inspired this thinking back in the 80's and 90's. Because of their high positions and since it was before deregulation, they skirted the law with inside information and became filthy rich. Both were rewarded with prison sentences and had to give most of the money back. If they had waited for a decade or so, this type of thinking would have taken them into the safe realm of "too big to fail," and they could have lived happily ever after and not in prison. Without regulation this game became so easy for those positioned well up the ladder.

Let's take a look at the other end of the spectrum. Jesus said, "Give a man a fish and you feed him for a day. Teach him to fish and you feed him for life." Jesus was for the people. Ivan, Michael, and Gordon were for themselves. Jesus felt good because He was helping people. Ivan, Michael and Gordon felt good because they felt they deserved all the money and the high position. They felt they deserved to be better than others; superior. They were on top looking down at all those that didn't have the "stuff" they did. All the others down there were not smart enough to see how they got up there. They felt others were inferior. They were bigots of the financial sort. Do I need to name others?

CHAPTER 24

Bigotry usually follows down a line of authority. This is the exact opposite of wealth. When it is heard coming from a lesser rank it can be passed off as ignorance. However, should bigotry be coming from one's boss, one tends to listen. If it's coming from a parent, teacher, preacher, officer, or politician, one not only tends to listen, one tends to be taught. Children are not born bigots. They are taught bigotry. If it is the standard thinking of your family, then you are taught to be a teacher of it.

Maya Angelou, one of my favorite people, said, "you don't have to think of doing the right thing if you are the right thing. People will forget what you say. People will forget what you do. They will never forget how you made them feel." Sometimes this damage is irreparable and separates indefinitely. Yet in this country, bigotry is common and practiced openly. Seldom is anything done about it because the offender can connect these hateful words upward.

Then along comes a black president, the perfect model of being human. Education, stature, reputation, and family, President Obama is in the mold of what an American should aspire to be. I can't imagine how he and his family feel as a result of the disrespectful attitude so openly expressed in the country he represents.

This is why Maya Angelou's words are so important. She, Martin Luther King, and other black leaders have been the backbone of the civil rights movement. White leaders have been present in this, but they just do not come readily to my mind and I do not wonder why. Black leaders have left many milestones along the way. Methods and laws have been left along this path.

Civil rights have been proven and documented by great thinkers, academics, and religious leaders since the 60's. Yet, it is necessary that this book be written over five decades later.

Hate groups have never been greater in numbers. It is my understanding that more than 2,000 hate groups exist in this country. Radical religious groups preach and practice racial hatred daily. Not too long ago, a Republican political leader spoke at a white supremacist convention. I will not give credence to this person or group by mentioning such names. And there you have it; radical political leaders find ways to keep this hatred in the forefront of the voting public.

A continuing repertoire is preached daily on Fox News Live. They highlight these leaders as the only real authority we have. Rush Limbaugh continues with his twenty million listeners daily. As our country becomes less educated (dumbed down), a huge portion of the population is a ready listener. They can spread this hate because our leaders acknowledge, condone, and preach it. As it follows down the chain of authority, it multiplies.

To those that lack proper family training and education causing the birth of this, it is well on the way to becoming explosive as noted in Mountain Home, Arkansas. Then we have periodic catastrophic uprisings as in Ferguson and Staten Island. Are these uprisings? Certainly; count the number of protesters. Are they wrong? Certainly not. Is the continuation of violence wrong? It certainly is.

CHAPTER 25

As we creep toward the cure I want to be careful, but I also want to be succinct. This is because we have many out there doing great work; going with everything they have and making some headway. I particularly wish to commend the Reverend Al Sharpton. He has risen to prominence with his daily show on MSNBC.

From out of the ghettos in early life, finding steps forward by every means and methods he could muster, showing courage regardless of the extreme opposition that was ever-present. Here he is now, proving his ability as an activist by presenting acts of racial inequality, and doing this without the slightest act of violence. Upon his head is placed the "crown of thorns" by those who question his right to do so.

The slander and degradation to him, his heritage, and his demeanor is about as radical and extreme as I have ever witnessed. I quote from a recent conversation about Ferguson: "This little 'n-word' with a big black head and slicked back hair is stirring up more violence by just being there." Terrible words, but so self-explanatory of racial hatred. Of course this came from an overweight stupid white man that probably didn't finish grade school. I don't know his name. I don't want to because what could a person say to him in response to this. I also didn't hear anyone refute these comments standing around him. My only thoughts while standing there were, *birds of a feather flock together*.

Is this not a fine example of seeds being cast about on fertile but spoiled soil? Is this not a fine example of reverse-activism heading in the wrong direction? Should I start with an explanation of his physical appearance and attire? Should I cast my seeds upon his soil? The answer is no. The damage is done. This would not cure anything and may create another act of violence. This was so aptly displayed by Martin Luther King many years ago. A non-violent stance is the first requirement. The next stance should include the proper diagnosis, followed with the right treatment.

CHAPTER 26

We seek treatment for the disease of racial hatred diagnosed many years ago, and left without a solution. Why is this? Research all you wish. Read as deeply as you choose. Draw the only conclusion possible. Extreme racial hatred should be treated as any other extreme hatred. The problem begins with a "sniffle or slight cough" leading to this disease but a mild medicine can't be taken. This disease is chronic and can lead to a terminal conclusion. So a minor case of this will undoubtedly get worse unless something is done about it.

Now, if a person continues to "hang out" with those who have varying cases it will probably get worse. Should they be able to "catch it" before it's necessary to be hospitalized, per chance it can be treated in an "out-patient" manner. We're told this can be done with psychotherapy. To date and in most cases, the victim—yes, the victim—is treated in this manner. The victim seeks help because the practice of bigotry and prejudice has caused damage that requires treatment.

This is very common in these days. The person that caused this damage seldom to never gets any kind of treatment because those around him have been carrying minor (to major) cases for many years. Just a nasty habit that somehow became acceptable behavior and later became a twisted sense of fun. Fun in that these people receive pleasure while watching others suffer. And there you have this vicious circle laced so deeply in our society. So deeply it can only be seen as twisted humor at the expense of others. Causing emotional damage to others and considered a method of making the self feel better. Did I paint that well? Are we there yet? Do you feel the pain of others? Do you now understand this disease? Do you think we should do something about it? Do you think our leaders, doctors, and preachers alike should treat this as any other hatred that may lead to a serious crime if it hasn't already?

CHAPTER 27

A quote from Michael Creighton from *State of Fear*: "Do you know what we call opinion in the absence of evidence? It is called prejudice." This is so true. The Native Americans were living here happily in their own culture on their own land. First we slaughter them and steal all their land. Then we force those still remaining into small parcels called reservations. Then we slander and degrade them because they don't quite fit into the way we do things. We rob, pilfer, and steal human cargo in another land and bring them here as slaves so we do not have to work and toil on this Indian land. Because they find a way toward a better life as free people, we slander and degrade them as they better themselves all the way to the presidency of this country. We continue to slander and degrade them, being most careful that they get no credit for their accomplishments.

The only reasoning behind this is sickness; a mental disorder that has blown up into a serious disease. A common therapy used in psychiatric treatment is "body swapping," or put another way, "walking in someone else's shoes." Let's try that: close your eyes and picture yourself as a slave, three fifths of a human being but treated as a farm animal with no rights whatsoever. Fed and clothed with the bare minimum. You work until you drop without any remuneration. Feel it? Understand where you are? Understand that you are owned as chattel and can be sold or traded as such? Understand that you cannot love or bear children that do not immediately become more chattel? Any form of self must be kept hidden and only shared with others whose skin is darker from the ones that own you. Feel it?

Open your eyes and try to better yourself from that position. The slave did this and aspired all the way to the top of this country. What did the owner do to help him? Now we are here and we have this history to look back on. Now we see how this darker-skinned person did this. Are we proud of this ascension? Are we proud that these people aspired and helped us build this country? Do we relish having them as our friends and neighbors? Do we admire them for these astonishing achievements?

If you can come up with a yes to those questions you just may not need treatment. Answer them "no", and *look out*, those people knocking on your door may have brought with them these cute little white canvas jackets that tie in the back. You may be on the way to the "funny farm." It was named this because you thought it was funny when you slandered and degraded certain people so you could feel better about yourself. Funny thing about this—it just may have something to do with that circle mentioned before.

Now picture yourself at a new starting line. Your Daddy didn't leave you a few million to get started with. The skin tones at this race run from light to dark. Start running! Guess who I placed my money on?

CHAPTER 28

Well, okay then. Let's imagine that we are all on top of this burning building. We are of all different skin tones; we are young and old, rich and poor. Everyone, that is, except for me. I'm on the ground with the net, and I just want to find out how much money I can get for it. After all, it's a free market, isn't it? "Anyone can jump in for a million dollars!" I yell. Alice Walton, Donald Trump, and Mitt Romney yell back, "how much for just three? We only have a million between us, and if we all jump and are all saved who will recognize the difference between us?" "Only God," I respond. I hear back, "when will he pay us back?" and I say, "when He meets you in heaven." Again, Alice, Don, and Mitt yell back, "what's the difference, we'll keep the million."

This is how the NWDP, which stands for "National White Dumb People," was founded. Our system has been "fixed," and the "fixers" have been paid by the NWDP. Now all we have to do is let our money make money. When this all ends just doesn't seem too damned important to us. Perhaps we can get the NWDP to fix that. Better yet, let our kids do it. They will be able to afford it. After all, look at the bundle we left them. It doesn't take brains to make money but it does take them to live. So let's move on.

Aluminum is a lightweight metal used to make beer cans, siding, and airplanes. Aluminum is often cast aside when empty, worn out, or obsolete. More often than not it ends up in dumps. Along comes a company named Novelis up in my neck of the woods in Oswego, New York. It's very cold up there with a lot of people out of work as their jobs moved overseas. Novelis hired a lot of these people who gathered up all this junk aluminum, recycled it, and sold it to Ford Motor Company to make the new 2015 Ford F-150 Pickup Truck. This truck is over 700 pounds lighter and gets far better mileage and is expected to sell better than the old model that already outsells every other car or truck made. That took brains.

My wife, Marilyn, doesn't particularly like this chapter. She says my humor is a bit too twisted and stupid to be funny. My answer was, "that's exactly what I'm trying to do. I'm just not as good at it as the NWDP."

CHAPTER 29

Okay, now for the scary stuff. Simply put, the people who run this country are very scary. When Speaker Boehner stands at the podium and speaks to us through the media, I wonder what he is thinking. I am always left with the feeling that he has an underlying meaning. Then he dashes from the podium when the last word is being spoken. Yes, it's just before the last couple of syllables.

We all know he is quick to tear up, smokes heavily, and so much has been written about his drinking habits. He also flips around quotes from Alcoholics Anonymous from time to time. I'm a fine one to be bringing this up because tonight at midnight, January 1, 2015, I celebrate forty-four years of sobriety. I'm rather proud of that, but by no means does this qualify me for being Speaker of the House or the questioner of someone's sobriety. What I am saying is, he always leaves me doubting his intentions. He is one of the biggest critics and questioners of respect when it comes to President Obama. I just don't trust the guy. He is third from the top and the boss congressman. There is always dissension in the ranks below him. He is always blocking the chance for the working class to advance. Now that the President is getting credit for lower gas prices, low unemployment rate, highest Dow Jones figures, best employment growth, and a few other things, Speaker Boehner is casting the accolades upon himself and other Republicans for these accomplishments.

As it has been said, "If President Obama could walk on water it would be because he can't swim." But—and it's very big but—I trust him. I trust his intentions. Sure, he is not perfect and may grab a ciggie now and then, but we have every right to trust him. Any slander or disrespect has been conjured up to hinder his reputation and to try to make him fail. Yes, we live in a country where the governing body called Congress wants him to fail. If he fails, we all fail. Speaker Boehner and the bunch he speaks for pulls no punches and clearly states this is their prime concern. *And you want me to trust him*?

CHAPTER 30

In this book, I have taken you over the hill and through the woods. I have cast aspersions in every direction I can think of. These doubts are hard to believe at times and then at other times, we begin believing the doubts. We doubt there is any chance to cure the greed and bigotry that have a very firm grasp on our country. I am firmly of the thought that if we remove greed, bigotry will be heading in the right direction to begin curing itself. Its purpose will be diminished. If we are treating everybody fairly and equally, what's the need for it?

Being greedy is the backbone of capitalism and I see little chance for this to change—the need for governing regulations has never been more paramount. If capitalism is not controlled it can be very destructive. Everything in the history of this country has proven this. Freewheeling capitalism is not free marketing. As free marketing gets misunderstood and capitalism runs wild, we head dangerously close to the apex of Maslow's pyramid. Should that happen, our dearly loved oligarchy becomes a kingdom.

Again Mr. Reagan, I wish to correct you. Government should not be the problem. Government is not the problem—your way of thinking is. The thinking that tolerating all the corruption that capitalism breeds will lead to sound government is pretty damned twisted, Mr. Reagan. Rest well and we do hope God has helped you with your thinking process.

Small government controlled by monstrously huge companies owned by the very few rich at the top is also not the answer. Nor is a corrupt huge government. All that has been accomplished here is twisting the middle to the extreme right or left. We must all fall back and rewind.

As a country we have proven we are unable to listen to President Obama. When he made his announcement address six years ago on those Illinois steps, he truly believed we would listen to his ideas of change and hope. Beautiful, well-spoken words, and he had my vote then. Oh yes, he had others as well, enough others to carry him all the way to the White House. Then others in his beloved system that he had hoped to lead set about destroying him.

In my lifetime I have never seen the likes and, at eighty-four, please spare me from doing this again. This has been the most disgusting display of adult actions ever witnessed. To me this goes beyond treasonous behavior. Treason condoned by our present legal system. Unbelievable behavior accepted by half of the population of this country. Unbelievable behavior readily displayed and practiced amongst a large portion of the voting public. Unbelievable behavior rooted in *bigotry*. And here we are at the purpose of this book.

CHAPTER 31

Please allow me to start with the opinion that fifty percent of our country will immediately think the pain of the cure exceeds the pain of the disease. No, that is not right. Fifty percent of the people in this country do not think they are diseased, therefore no cure is necessary. This fifty percent thinks this hatred running through their veins is normal and it is people like me that disrupt this so-called normalcy. Moreover, by the mere fact of writing this book, it could cause my termination. It could also create the need for immediate relocation.

Authors hope that all will read and enjoy their work. This is certainly not in my plans, nor is getting lynched. My only hope is that this book may highlight the things that may lead to a path toward a more peaceful and self-replenishing country. I am foolish enough to think so. This book is certainly not doing this now and it hasn't for more years than I wish to count.

Let's get on with it. Churches of nearly all denominations differ in some way. It seems that most churches are Protestant. That word, in itself, lights the first fire. To protest is to differ; to differ leads to discussion. Discussions have led to arguments, and eventually heated arguments have led to wars—one way or another. Is it necessary to delve into history, or can you accept that religion has caused just about every war?

Re-legioning is to convert. To re-legion or convert. One believes one way, one believes the other. There is only one answer to this question. Believe as you wish. Just don't argue about it. Keep re-legioning and conversion out of it. For those that may wonder, that means religion. This is the major cause of these wars. A difference of opinion should never be "cast in stone". God made everybody. Please leave His work alone. He is happy with it and, therefore, we all should be.

RULE #1, never belong to a church that does not accept everyone regardless of opinion, race, sexual orientation, or gender.

RULE #2, don't belong to any organization that does.

RULE #3, believe all people are created equal and treat them equally under the law. Simply do not break this law.

RULE #4, don't make it necessary to make up any more of these damned rules.

This leaves us with deciding whom we will vote for. Let's just accept that having a system of government beats anarchy. Even in a losing game, oligarchy beats anarchy. Let's not rush further to the rear. There just isn't much time left. A governing system can be self-leveling, self-perpetuating, and even peaceful toward all people and constituents. Take a look up in Scandinavia. Not perfect, but heading in the right direction. We just haven't been playing the game that way. God only knows why?

Every evening we get to watch some other countries settle their debates by flinging gavels, books, and furniture at each other. Others spend more on uniforms for little tin soldiers to march in threatening parades so other countries will notice how threatening they are. Our lessons are put in front of us. We accept these lessons as a method to determine how we should vote. Now watch—listen very carefully—*do you vote*? It's your only chance. It's our only chance. Don't blow it; *do it*! No excuses—DO IT! VOTE!

Now I will begin telling you how to go about this. Please don't argue with me, chase me out of town, or shoot me. Just hear this opinion and tell me you understand it and then I will hear and understand yours. No, I will not argue, chase you out of town, or shoot you.

Listen deeply to the TV and radio commentators. Read everything you can get your hands on. Listen to all of those around you. Then vote for the candidate that has most closely obeyed those four rules. Believe me, you can't go wrong, and you will be doing your part to repair and recreate a country we will all want to live in. You can make all the changes you want to. You can create as much hope as you wish and never depart from those rules.

Now, if your candidate was a corrupt, thieving crook in office before, he can still be one under those rules. Those rules or any other will not keep him from being re-elected if you don't vote. This is where the brains come in, like Novelis used. You remember them don't you? It doesn't cost you anything to use them but even if it did, those dollars are already spent. That's yesterday's newspaper. You've heard that song before.

Today's newspaper advised that Mr. Huckabee has resigned from Fox News so he can decide about his chances to be president. It is he who refers to the "secular left" as being Godless and without faith. It is he who champions others to follow toward the "religious right" and forfeit thoughts of global warming, the right to choose, or any other scientific thought that may redirect intellectual or philosophical points of view. This type of thinking could possibly lead to change, and Mr. Huckabee doesn't want that.

My thoughts may seem a bit secular about religion, but they are not. The intention is meant to clearly not align with any group rooted in any form of hate. Your eyes have been opened to four little rules that lead to the study of your fellow man and you have learned to like him. All of them, crooks alike, and you like them all. If you use your brains, study and think, you will know who is corrupt and twisted. You just are no longer going to toss your vote away and vote for those that fit that mold. You will want to get them out of office, out of the way or maybe in jail where they truly belong. Yes, you can like them through the bars on the back of a paddy wagon.

Whew! So far I don't see any pickups with shotguns in the back windows in my driveway. It might be a good time to end this chapter.

CHAPTER 32

I awake for another day. I'm still here, still willing to keep my nose heading in the right direction. Still searching for a free and peaceful existence amongst all of you. Come on over and sit under my awning this summer in upstate New York. The coffee will be strong and hot. The flowers will be starting to bloom and the baby ducks will come to be fed. Boats will be put in the water all spiffed up and shining brightly. Conversations will be starting about the coming presidential primaries and elections.

What an opportunity to practice these four rules. What an opportunity to be amongst my friends, who are all of different opinions, different in all the aforementioned ways. We are all different and we are all alike. We are all children of God and He didn't make any mistakes. It is only we who still misunderstand Him, and therefore it is us who make the mistakes. We can talk about that. We can talk about anything—we can differ, we just shouldn't argue; the other guy just may be right.

And, even if he isn't right, his views are important. Your views are important. Your views may change and his may also. *But*, it will be his choice, your choice. His choice to vote however he wishes and that is what makes the world go around. As it spins, we learn, we study, we listen, and it is only in these methods that we can learn how to be wrong peacefully, with a complete understanding of how we got to be wrong. Understanding that the other guy just may be right. Gracefully, we accept each other as an important part of being human. Gratefully, we are to be here upon this earth for just a short time, together and not alone.

I am sure I will be faulted for my display of a quick understanding of churches and religion. I apologize and wish to be forgiven. It was done to arrive at a crescendo; to arouse your interest and to prompt thoughts; your thoughts and not mine. An understanding of theology alone has always left me feeling that I'm getting only part of the story.

Great philosophers that came along after Jesus stirred my beliefs leaving me with a faith, as I understand it. That alone came along in 1935 by Bill Wilson, the founder of Alcoholics Anonymous. Forty-four years without a drink has confirmed it for me. Others have contributed to this faith. Epictetus, a Greek philosopher that died 135 years after Christ, ranks way up there for me. If you have read my last book, *How Ed Was Made*, it clearly defines that I am not educated, as such.

Those that left me with only a reasonable facsimile have taught me. Just enough to make me chase down people like Epictetus. It was he, a slave, who said, "only the educated are free." As he aspired he said, "Wealth consists not of having great possessions. It consists of having few wants. Hopes of the instructed far exceed the wealth of the ignorant."

I sit here, near eighty-four years of age and wonder how it happened. How did I get this old? Why do I think the way that I do? Why is my thinking different from those around me? Why are those around still teaching me? Why is it those still around me appear to be still learning? Ask Epictetus; I did and I still do. He was just a slave as a child but fortunate enough to be taught by those around him. He was taught enough to be still learning, though quite a teacher at his death in 135 AD.

EPILOGUE

I have a dear friend near the Arkansas and Missouri border. He came into my life in 1948 aboard the USS Brush DD-745. We fought together, we lived together, and we also experienced racial bigotry and prejudice in a very segregated U.S. Navy. This was sixty-five years ago. We have remained close friends and, yes, we still think the same. We also think our country has not changed. It has had its ups and downs, but at its heart, the base cause for civil rights is deeply imbedded in our society and culture.

Great work is being done by the likes of Mark Potok of the Southern Poverty Law Center. We have had some superior black leaders